Why Do I Feel Uneasy?

Why Do I Feel Uneasy?

More Cartoons
by Pat Oliphant

Andrews and McMeel
A Universal Press Syndicate Company
Kansas City

'IT'S MR. ALLEN — HE HAS AN IDEA FOR A MOVIE.'

'DON'T QUOTE ME ON THIS, BUT THESE HURRICANES ARE CAUSED BY GODLESS, NON-CHRISTIAN, PRO-CHOICE, ANTI-FAMILY, HOMOSEXUAL-SYMPATHIZING, LIBERAL, UNPATRIOTIC, PRO-CLINTON PREVERTS!'

THE ROAD TO MAASTRICHT.

PASS THE BABY

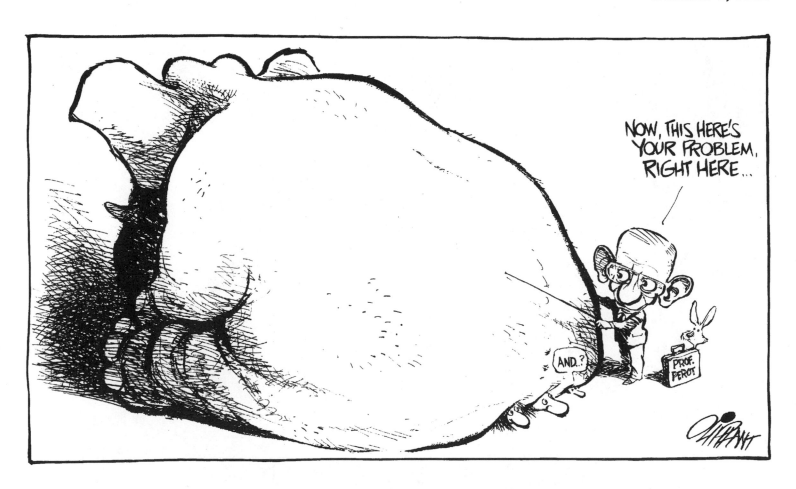

October 9, 1992

AND NOW, THE MODERATOR OF THIS FIRST DEBATE...

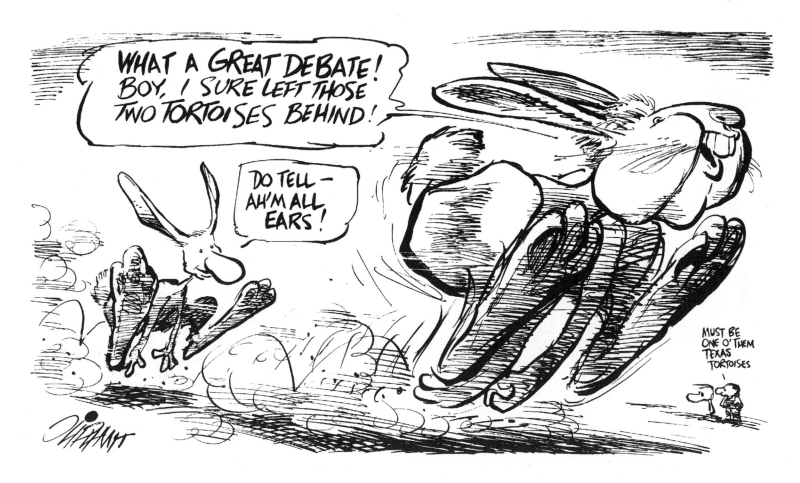

SLOW DANCING

GEORGE BUSH, BILL CLINTON AND ROSS PEROT SHARE THE 1992 NOBEL PIES FOR POLITICAL DEBATE (ADMIRAL STOCKDALE ACCEPTING FOR MR. PEROT.)

A DISRUPTED WEDDING.

MARKS OF PROGRESS IN AMERICAN BUSINESS.

MEANWHILE, BACK IN THE REST OF THE WORLD...

'EITHER ALL OUR CHICKENS CAME HOME TO ROOST, OR THIS IS THE ARKANSAS TRANSITION TEAM.'

November 13, 1992

37

'DEAR MOM. WELL, HERE I AM IN THIS FOXHOLE WITH MY TWO BUDDIES, LURLENE AND BRUCE. I DO NOT APPEAR TO BE IN ANY IMMEDIATE DANGER...'

SOCKS GOES TO WASHINGTON.

NOW AND THEN, A SECRET SERVICE AGENT WILL LOSE IT.

49

'I WISH SOMEONE WOULD DO SOMETHING ABOUT THOSE DARN AX-MURDERERS NEXT DOOR!'

'BUT I ONLY PARDONED THOSE PEOPLE TO DEMONSTRATE HOW COMPLETELY OUT-OF-TOUCH I REALLY AM!'

January 7, 1993

'WHAT'S ALL THE FUSS ABOUT CHELSEA? IF I HAD MY DRUTHERS I'D GO TO A PRIVATE SCHOOL MY OWNSELF.'

SECOND-HAND SMOKE.

SLOW LEARNER.

BIG ROCK, LITTLE ROCK.

'...BUT FIRST, THE PRESSING ISSUE OF GAYS IN THE MILITARY.'

THE RETURN OF SLICK WILLIE.

'I SUPPOSE A HONEYMOON IS OUT OF THE QUESTION?'

February 4, 1993

73

'IT'S POLITICAL CORRECTNESS GONE MAD — THE OLD NAME NOW APPLIES TO THE REST OF THE CITY ONLY!'

`HELLO, ATTORNEY GENERAL SPEAKING!`

'HONEST, I DIDN'T KNOW HE WAS THIS BIG — I SWEAR I DIDN'T!'

THE PLAN.

O'LEARY SQUINTED DOWN THE BAR TO SEE WHO HAD ORDERED THE PINK GIN. SOON
AFTER THIS, THE LIGHTS WENT OUT.

'I PERFORMED IN TIME OF CRISIS WID POISE, ASSURANCE AND IMPERTURBABLE SELF-POSSESSION, DEY SAID. FURTHER, I EXHIBITED GREAT SAVOIR-FAIRE AND APLOMB, DEY SAID. I TOLD 'EM TO GO STUFF IT!'

SO THEY DROPPED HIM ON BOSNIA.

March 10, 1993

89

THE RIGHT·TO·LIFERS HAVE SPOKEN.

WARFARE JUST AIN'T WHAT IT USED TO BE.

NINE LIVES AND COUNTING...

'OK, YOU TELL HIM HE CAN'T COME ON PATROL WITH US BECAUSE HE'S A HOMOSEXUAL!'

April 8, 1993

'OLGA! OLGA! IS RICH NATIONS' CLEARINGHOUSE SWEEPSTAKES! WE MAY HAVE ALREADY WON 28 BILLION DOLLARS!'

April 26, 1993

111

'AS FOR REPAIRING THE REST OF OUR IMAGE, I HAVE NO IDEA...'

'THAT'S IT, BILL—ALWAYS LET HIM KNOW WHO'S IN CHARGE!'

April 30, 1993

AMERICANS WELCOME.

'NOW HEAR THIS. THE SENATOR IS HERE TO STUDY FIRST-HAND THE CLOSE-QUARTER SLEEPING ARRANGEMENTS ABOARD SUBMARINES, YOU WILL ASSIST THE SENATOR. NOW MOVE OVER.'

IN NEW YORK A KID, POSING AS A MOTORMAN, STOLE A SUBWAY TRAIN AND DROVE IT ALL OVER HELL AND GONE. SIMILARLY, IN WASHINGTON, ...

GUARD DUTY.

MALE EMPLOYEE AWARDED ONE MILLION DOLLARS IN SEXUAL HARASSMENT SUIT.

May 28 1993

'PAY IT NO MIND. IT'S ONLY MIDDLE-MANAGEMENT.'

'LET'S COMPROMISE, GENERAL — WE'LL BOTH PICK IT UP.'

June 2, 1993

132

June 3, 1993

'MR. GERGEN, THERE'S A GROWN-UP TO SEE YOU. SAYS HE'S TANNED, RESTED AND READY.
SAYS YOU'D KNOW WHAT THAT MEANS... MR. GERGEN, LIKE AM I MISSING SOMETHING...?'

133

'REWRITE ON YOUR TIRED, YOUR POOR, YOUR HUDDLED, ETC..!'

"YOU CALLED ME A GAY-LOVING, DRAFT-DODGING, POT-SMOKING WOMANIZER." HE SAYS. "YOU OWE ME AN APOLOGY!" "HEY, YOU'RE RIGHT, SIR," I SAYS. "I FORGOT YOU DIDN'T INHALE!"

IN LATER YEARS IT WOULD BE KNOWN AS "THE AARP INTERCEPT".

CLINTON PARK.

'A GOODWILL GESTURE FROM PRESIDENT CLINTON — WHERE SHOULD I PUT IT?'

'WHAT'S WRONG WITH THESE PEOPLE? OBVIOUSLY THEY HAVE THAT NAVAJO DISEASE, OR SOMETHING.'

'SO... LET'S SEE YOU ROW.'

TWO-PARTY SYSTEM: PHASE I.

June 29, 1993

OK, SADDAM – LET THAT BE A LESSON TO YOU AND YOUR KIND!
BIP
WADDEE SAY?
HE SAYS YOU ARE FREE TO STAY HERE ILLEGALLY, AND KILL WHOMEVER YOU PLEASE, O GREAT ONE.
BOMB PLANS
THE GLOVES SOMEWHAT MUFFLE THE MESSAGE.

'I SAY WE SPRAY 'EM, AND SCREW THE LONG-TERM HAZARDS!'

July 7, 1993

`THAT, TO BEGIN WITH, IS NOT A VERY HELPFUL ATTITUDE, MR. MIYAZAWA!`

148

July 9, 1993

THE CLINTON EFFECT ON JAPANESE BUSINESSMEN HAS STILL TO BE CALCULATED.

150

July 14, 1993

'NO, MA'AM, THERE'S NO CAUSE FOR ALARM — THE CORPS LICKED THE MIGHTY MISSISSIPPI YEARS
AGO... YES, MA'AM, REST ASSURED THAT YOUR ARMY ENGINEERS KNOW THEIR BUSINESS...'

'IT'S A DISGRACE THE WAY THE WHOLE LAW PROFESSION IS MALIGNED THESE DAYS—WHY, I'M GOING TO LODGE A FORMAL COMPLAINT WITH THE LAWYERS' ANTI-DEFAMATION LEAGUE!'

'HAVE A NICE VISIT, REVEREND.'